25 APARTMENTS & LOFTS

UNDER 2500 SQUARE FEET

25 APARTMENTS & LOFTS
UNDER 2500 SQUARE FEET

JAMES GRAYSON TRULOVE

COLLINS | DESIGN

An Imprint of HarperCollinsPublishers

25 APARTMENTS AND LOFTS UNDER 2500 SQUARE FEET

HarperCollins books may be purchased for educational, business, or sales promotional use.
For information, please write: Special Markets Department, HarperCollins Publishers,
10 East 53rd Street, New York, NY 10022.

First published in 2006 by:
Collins Design
An Imprint of HarperCollins*Publishers*
10 East 53rd Street
New York, NY 10022
Tel: (212) 207-7000
Fax: (212) 207-7654
collinsdesign@harpercollins.com
www.harpercollins.com

Distributed throughout the world by:
HarperCollins*Publishers*
10 East 53rd Street
New York, NY 10022
Fax: (212) 207-7654

Packaged by:
Grayson Publishing, LLC
James G. Trulove, Publisher
1250 28th Street NW
Washington, DC 20007
202-337-1380
jtrulove@aol.com
Design and Art Direction by: Agnieszka Stachowicz

Library of Congress Control Number: 2006930942

ISBN-10: 0-06-114989-6
ISBN-13: 978-0-06-11498-4

Manufactured in China
First printing, 2006
1 2 3 4 5 6 7 8 9 / 08 07 06 05

CONTENTS

Foreword		6
5th Avenue Duplex	New York	12
Perlman Apartment	New York	20
Beale Street Residence	San Francisco	30
Arnold Residence	Denver	40
Cady's Alley Apartment	Washington, DC	48
Park Avenue Corner	New York	58
Lujan Apartment	Washington, DC	68
Mercer Street Loft	New York	76
Stoll Apartment	Washington, DC	84
Sullivan Street Loft	New York	92
Meatpacking District Loft	New York	102
Kellner Loft	New York	110
SoHo Duplex	New York	120
White Street Loft	New York	128
Bernhardt Residence	Denver	136
Atherley Loft	New York	144
Gardner Loft	New York	152
19th Street Loft	New York	162
Morgan Loft	New York	170
Chelsea Apartment	New York	178
Zartoshty Residence	Boston	186
Gordon SoHo Skyline Loft	New York	194
Midtown Triplex	New York	202
Capps Loft	San Antonio, TX	210
Collins Loft	New York	218

FOREWORD

APARTMENTS ARE BECOMING INCREASINGLY POPULAR AS empty-nesters, suburbanites, young singles, and couples opt for the commute-free urban life. Once-dead inner cities across the U.S. are bustling with life as old, long-empty industrial buildings become live/work lofts and new high-style condominiums sprout in lots where weeds once grew. As the cost of residential real estate continues to soar, existing apartments are being renovated to a high standard, reflecting their increased value.

Throughout all this construction and renovation, if a single trend can be identified in apartment design, whether new construction or renovation, the key word is "open." Many of the apartments in this book have a loft-like ambiance: owners seek to combine living, dining, and cooking areas into large expanses for more informal entertaining and socializing. Elsewhere in the home, sliding partitions replace fixed walls to allow the flexible use of space. Translucent glass and plastics envelop bathrooms, giving these once strictly private spaces of the home a communal, spalike appearance.

As for materials, many of the projects in this book feature glass, plastic, steel, and stone. Architects and their clients use them to create a more modern, industrial appearance. is one reason. Also the translucence of sand-blasted glass or many plastic laminates allow architects to bring natural light deep into windowless areas.

There are, of course, more traditional approaches to apartment design but even in these cases, we can see innovative methods for creating more efficient, dramatic space. All in all, the twenty-five apartments featured here serve as an excellent cross-section of current interior design in new apartments and condominiums.

ABOVE: Open stairs and etched glass walls contribute to a light, airy interior in the Beale Street Loft. RIGHT: The Morgan Loft is distinguished by its vaulted clay-brick ceilings.

LEFT: Prefabricated sheet-metal forms enabled the Gardner Loft to be completed in a month.

ABOVE: Although located in the back of the building, the Lujan Apartment is bathed in light thanks to a deep skylight over the living area.

LEFT: Floor-to-ceiling windows and an outdoor terrace bring the outdoors into the Cady's Alley apartment.

BELOW: Open spaces (complete with see-through stairs) make the Capps Loft ideal for a collector of modern art.

PROJECTS

5TH AVENUE DUPLEX

ARCHITECTS MAYA LIN STUDIO/DAVID HOTSON ARCHITECT • PHOTOGRAPHERS PAUL WARCHOL/MICHAEL MORAN

2100 SQUARE FEET

THE PRINCIPAL CHALLENGE POSED BY THIS RENOVATION PROJECT was to create a serene, luminous space in an existing two-story apartment where the main living area is located below ground level.

From the building lobby one enters the apartment directly on the stair landing between the two floors. The living, dining, and kitchen areas are located on the larger lower level. The entry space is sheathed in warm sycamore paneling, connecting the two floor levels, opening vistas through the apartment and distributing natural light to the interior bathrooms through etched glass partitions.

A sliding partition converts the upper-level bathroom into two self-contained bathrooms with independent entrances. A pivoting wardrobe cabinet converts the second sleeping area from a spacious guest room into two children's bedrooms.

Similar transformable elements recur throughout the apartment. Appliances are hidden behind sycamore cabinets, allowing the kitchen to serve as an uncluttered background for the dining area. The simple island cabinet in the kitchen conceals four chairs.

Floor Plan

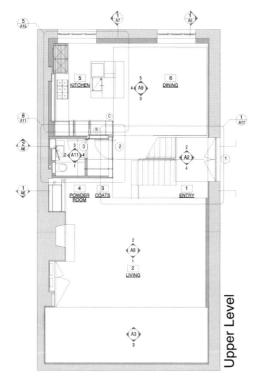

Upper Level

Lower Level

PREVIOUS PAGES: The apartment
is entered at the stair landing,
between the two floors. Here,
the stair is seen from the living
room on the lower level.

RIGHT: The kitchen island
conceals seating for a family
of four.
BELOW: An etched glass
partition separates the kitchen
from an interior bathroom.

FAR LEFT AND LEFT: Sycamore paneling covers the walls.

ABOVE AND RIGHT: Sliding partitions convert the luxurious single bath on the second floor into two fully independent baths.
LEFT: Master bedroom

PERLMAN APARTMENT

ARCHITECT AJS DESIGNS • PHOTOGRAPHER BJÖRG MAGNEA

2500 SQUARE FEET

THE GOAL FOR THE RENOVATION OF THIS APARTMENT WAS TO make the space feel more expansive. The wall that separated the living area from the master suite was removed, opening up the southern window wall. The kitchen moved from the center to the rear of the plan, opening up the front of the apartment. The master and guest bedrooms and bathrooms stayed in place, although the entrances and size of each space were modified, freeing up enough space for an additional half-bath and a laundry area.

Once the primary living areas were established, an open walnut spine was inserted into the design to house the owner's work area and to provide storage for books, music, and the media system. This centerpiece can be seen as part corridor, part screen and part pavilion. The spine also conceals or screens the apartment's service areas. Adjacent movable doors in the center of the spine and in the master bedroom create privacy when needed.

Finishing materials were chosen for their depth, warmth, and durability. Wide-plank ash floors laid east-west carry the eye along the window line and emphasize the width of the space while walnut veneers applied horizontally to walls and cabinets emphasize the length. The bathrooms were covered floor to ceiling in glass tile or cork to envelop the occupant.

PREVIOUS PAGES: View of the dining area and kitchen with the walnut spine at left
RIGHT: The living room with stone fireplace

Floor Plan

Existing Floor Plan

Sliding Screen in Open Position

Sliding Screen in Closed Position

FAR LEFT: The kitchen was significantly expanded.
LEFT: The open hallway contains bookcases and the office space

ABOVE LEFT AND LEFT: The perforated stainless steel screen, in the open and closed position in front of the work station RIGHT: A view of the master bedroom from the living area

LEFT: The master bathroom
with glass tiles
BELOW LEFT: The powder room
has cork walls and floors.
RIGHT: The master bedroom

BEALE STREET RESIDENCE

ARCHITECT AIDLIN DARLING DESIGN • PHOTOGRAPHER JOHN SUTTON

2500 SQUARE FEET

THE TECH-SAVVY CLIENT FOR THIS PROJECT REQUESTED THAT A claustrophobic loft space be opened up to show a significant art collection as well as embrace the spirit of the original warehouse.

The first step was to remove as many walls as possible, revealing an array of existing concrete columns. Bathrooms were grouped in the center of the plan in a neutrally defined enclosure that provides a backdrop for the gallery space on the lower level. When they are open, strategically located cabinets enable various areas to serve as the kitchen, living room, library, and study. When closed, they function as sculptural masses, two of which cut into the ceiling plane, providing portals for the sun. A floating maple staircase and adjacent two-story translucent glass wall connect the private first floor to the public second floor and the sky above: the pane refracts natural light and energizes the center of the loft on both levels. Downstairs, the raised maple floor with integrated floor lights warms up the more intimate spaces while providing a necessary raceway for computer infrastructure.

Overall, the design creates pockets of intimacy within the open plan. By integrating natural light and highly crafted wood interventions, this balanced environment complements the art collection.

ABOVE: The dining room
RIGHT: The maple floor on the lower level is raised to accommodate wiring for the computer infrastructure

Floor Plan

Upper Level

Lower Level

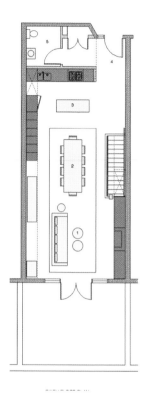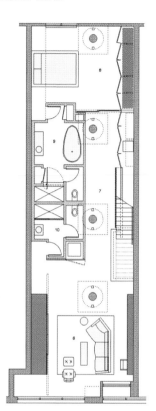

Stair Section

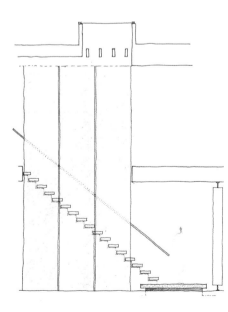

BELOW: Stair detail
RIGHT: The floating glass pane visually connects the two floors of the apartment.

FAR LEFT: The kitchen
LEFT: The fireplace in the second-floor living area; the primary finishing materials for the apartment are sand-blasted glass, stainless steel, and cherrywood cabinetry.

LEFT AND RIGHT: Workstation
and lower-level bookcases

ABOVE: Master bath
LEFT: First-floor family room

ARNOLD RESIDENCE

ARCHITECT **SIMPLE BROWN DESIGN** • PHOTOGRAPHER **RON POLLARD**

1525 **SQUARE FEET**

THIS URBAN GETAWAY HOME PROVIDES ITS OWNERS WITH A GREAT deal of flexibility for entertaining and daily activities. It features custom furniture, a bold palette of colors and materials, and an efficient layout that maximizes the living area.

The rough timber frame and brick walls were retained to contrast with the sleek panels of glass, metal and wood, and the brightly hued laminates. The historic structure provides rhythm and texture, while the contemporary materials generate energy and color. Blending the two styles are several custom tables: though made of the wood and metal from the building's original frame, they are contemporary in design. Dividing the loft is a linear spine by a wall of sliding and fixed panels made of glass and medium-density fiberboard. This wall separates the residence's public and private zones, while also providing built-in storage units. In addition, the rolling doors and translucent panels create interplay: open vs. closed, visible vs. covered, and clear vs. opaque.

The public spaces are positioned to take advantage of exterior light. Glass panels allow tempered, borrowed daylight into the private spaces. The kitchen and dining areas include backlit shelving for displaying the client's collection of glass objects.

PREVIOUS PAGES: A view of the
bedrooms from the kitchen area
BELOW: A serving bar

RIGHT: A detail of the sliding
and fixed doors separating the
bedrooms from the main living area

Mezzanine

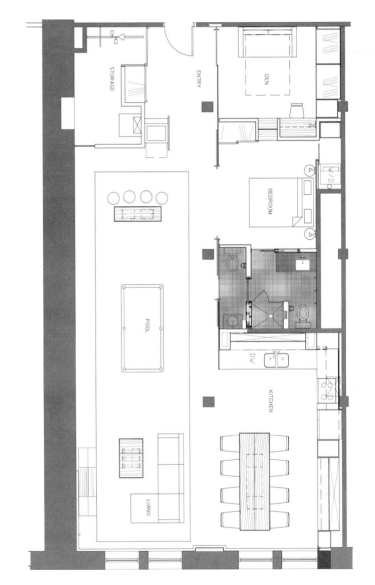

LEFT: A corridor separates the living and kitchen areas from the private quarters.
ABOVE: A backlit display niche in the kitchen holds the owners' glassware collection.

ABOVE RIGHT: A detail of the existing support beam in the renovated space

CADY'S ALLEY APARTMENT

ARCHITECT **FRANK SCHLESINGER ASSOCIATES ARCHITECTS** • PHOTOGRAPHER **JULIA HEINE**

2500 **SQUARE FEET**

THE BASIC ORGANIZATIONAL STRATEGY FOR THE APARTMENT was to arrange its main spaces—living room, dining room, and master bedroom—around the large, south-facing terrace overlooking the C&O Canal in Washington, DC's historic Georgetown.

The main living area is topped with a barrel vault. This was installed in response to a zoning restriction that would have limited the ceiling height to eight feet. However, vaults and domes are considered "embellishments" by local zoning ordinances and hence are not subject to this restriction. This interpretation allowed the architect to erect a dramatic barrel vault as the apartment's spatial armature.

The vault is covered with wood strips to provide visual texture as well as to counter any acoustic problems that result from its shape. The space is anchored at one end by a freestanding fireplace and at the other end by the open kitchen. The living area receives morning and evening light through deep slot windows at each end of the vault and south light via glass doors to the adjoining terrace. Painting the space white reinforces its plastic vitality and the quality of this natural light.

PREVIOUS PAGES: The living
room adjoins a terrace to the right.
RIGHT: The terrace overlooks the
C&O Canal below.

Floor Plan

Section

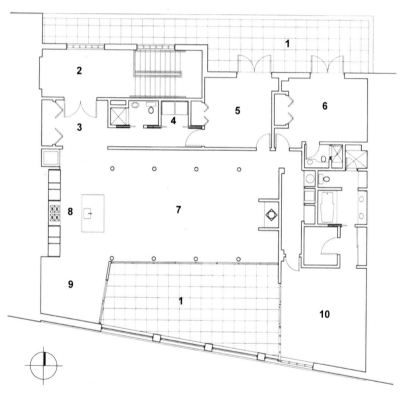

1 Terrace
2 Entry Stair
3 Foyer
4 Laundry
5 Bedroom/ Study
6 Bedroom
7 Great Room
8 Kitchen
9 Dining
10 Master Bedrrom

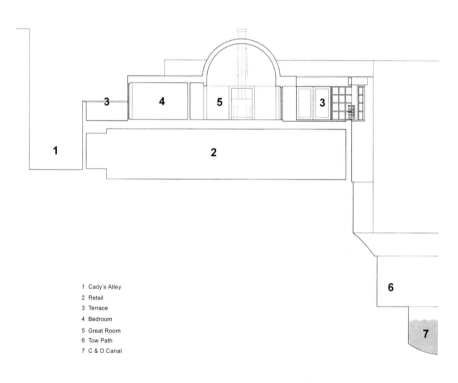

1 Cady's Alley
2 Retail
3 Terrace
4 Bedroom
5 Great Room
6 Tow Path
7 C & O Canal

FAR LEFT: The apartment wraps around the terrace, giving the master bedroom direct access to the outdoor space.

LEFT : Exterior views of the apartment showing the vaulted ceiling and the terrace

RIGHT: A view of the kitchen from the dining area
FAR RIGHT: A view of the dining area and kitchen from the living area
FOLLOWING PAGES: The living room and terrace

PARK AVENUE CORNER

ARCHITECT **CHELSEA ATELIER** • PHOTOGRAPHER **BJÖRG MAGNEA**

2500 SQUARE FEET

THIS LOFT IS LOCATED ON THE SOUTHEAST CORNER OF ITS BUILDING
and large windows flood the space with daylight. In the center is a
freestanding kitchen with an open ceiling, completely disengaged from
the surrounding structures of the loft. It overlooks the living/dining
area, where walls at either end stand before large fields of glass,
creating dramatic backdrops for art. The glass walls allow light to
penetrate deep into the loft. Their acid-etched texture diffuses the light
and reduces the need for frequent cleaning, since fingerprints do not
show on the rough surface.

The master bedroom and the spalike master bathroom occupy
one end of the loft while the guest bedrooms and exercise room cluster
at the other. The apartment's entrance is at one end of a generous
gallery that wraps around the kitchen. Floor-to-ceiling door frames
emphasize the verticality of the space.

Floor Plan

PREVIOUS PAGES: The living area's etched glass wall helps create a backdrop for paintings.

RIGHT: With its open ceiling, the island-like kitchen serves as the hub of the apartment.

Computer Model

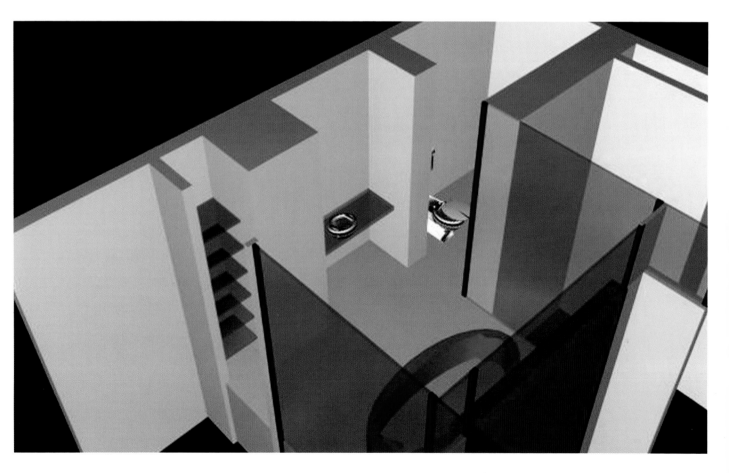

LEFT: Living, dining, and kitchen areas; etched glass walls allow light to penetrate deep into the apartment.

BELOW AND RIGHT: Acid-etched glass doors provide privacy for the spalike master bath while allowing light into the space.

FOLLOWING PAGES: Large perimeter windows flood the living room with light.

LUJAN APARTMENT

ARCHITECT **ROBERT M. GURNEY** • PHOTOGRAPHER **ANICE HOACHLANDER**

1500 **SQUARE FEET**

LOCATED ABOVE A BAKERY, THIS SECOND-FLOOR APARTMENT occupies the rear of the building. The space is accessible through a narrow ground-level doorway in an alley. A small foyer and closet are also on the ground level.

The space, originally used as a storage area, had never been renovated. It comprised two areas, separated by a 12-inch-thick brick wall with a 30-inch difference in floor height. Since the building is in a designated historic area, its exterior could be restored but not altered. Into existing window openings went new mahogany, double-hung windows with prescribed muntin profiles, sizes and configurations.

After renovation, an open space on the lower level contains the kitchen and living-area. Corrugated Galvalume panels sheathe the roof's sloping underside. A floating maple-paneled ceiling is suspended from that sloping surface to define and enrich the living and dining area.

A steel and aluminum stair rises to a new opening in the brick wall, a doorway to the elevated area, which now contains a bedroom, dressing room, bathroom, and small office.

Floor Plan

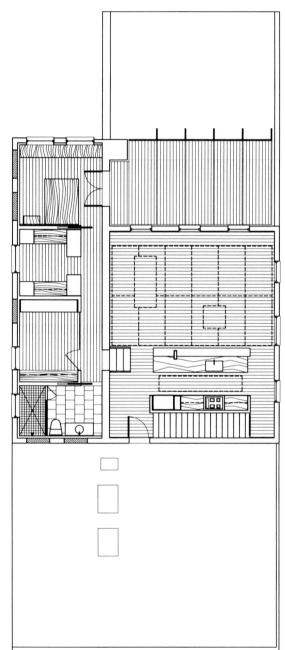

PREVIOUS PAGES: The living/dining, and kitchen
BELOW AND RIGHT: Three skylights with deep mahogany wells that extends below the maple ceiling panels are positioned to illuminate the entire space.

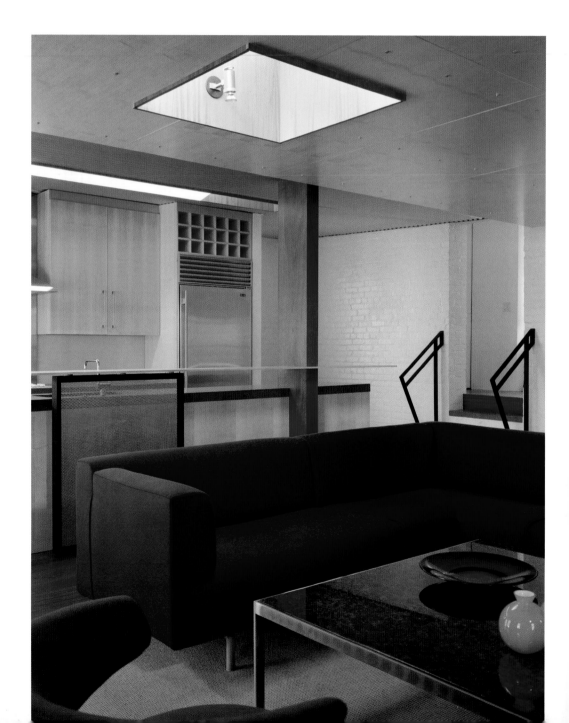

LEFT: Corrugated Galvalume panels in the kitchen allude to the industrial origins of this space.

ABOVE: Rich mahogany and maple millwork gives the apartment a feeling of warmth.

ABOVE: A view past the dressing-area closets toward the master bathroom

ABOVE RIGHT: Master bathroom
FAR RIGHT: A floating maple ceiling defines the living and dining area.

MERCER STREET LOFT

ARCHITECT **PULLTAB DESIGN** • PHOTOGRAPHER **EDUARD HUEBER ARCHPHOTO**

2300 SQUARE FEET

THE MOST PROMINENT FEATURE OF THIS LOFT IS THE THICKENED millwork surface that creates a continuous plane along the entry wall. It is constructed of rift-sawn white oak all milled from one tree. Behind it are storage and utility spaces. It also encloses a small vestibule off the elevator where guests can sit to take off shoes and hang up coats before entering the apartment.

The fireplace and chimney are clad in tinted, precast concrete panels. Centered above the fireplace is a plasma television, mounted flush with the face of the concrete. In the kitchen, the rift-oak breakfast countertop climbs the wall, becoming open shelving, and then turns down to envelop the base cabinetry. Since the kitchen does not have a window, the architect brought light into the space by creating an illuminated backsplash behind the sink using three-quarter-inch glass mosaic tiles. The fourteen-foot ceilings of the main space are punctuated by custom pendant light fixtures made by local SoHo artisans.

Floor Plan

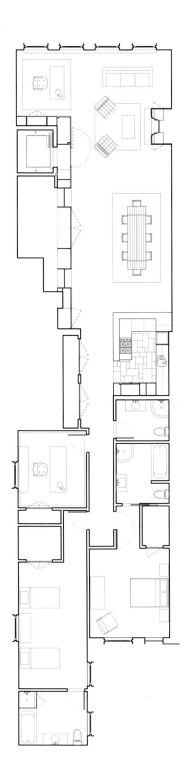

PREVIOUS PAGES: The white oak storage and entry wall extends from the kitchen area to the living area as a continuous plane.

BELOW: View from the entry.
RIGHT: Large, street-side windows flood the living area with natural light.

LEFT: View of the dining area and kitchen from the living area

BELOW: Three-quarter-inch glass tiles were used in the kitchen to reflect more light into the windowless space.

BELOW AND RIGHT: The entry
wall creates a continuous plane
that unifies the disparate elements of the loft.

STOLL APARTMENT

ARCHITECT **MCINTURFF ARCHITECTS** • PHOTOGRAPHER **JULIA HEINE**

2500 **SQUARE FEET**

BUILT IN 1905, THE BEAUX-ARTS EDIFICE IN WHICH THIS APARTMENT is located was erected during Washington, D.C.'s early 20th-century expansion up Connecticut Avenue. It is one of a series of grand urban apartment buildings from that era.

When the building was renovated in the 1970s, this fifth-floor unit was created by combining one full apartment with part of another. The result was a warren of small, poorly lit, disconnected rooms in which circulation was difficult. After the owners' purchase, the architects opened the kitchen to the adjacent living and dining areas, creating a large open space to take advantage of northern views. The entry was restructured, with a series of freestanding planes and cutout soffits defining path and place. The original windowless dining room was converted into a library. Throughout, lighting, color, and materials have been selected to gracefully introduce a modern spatial approach into this traditional building.

Floor Plan

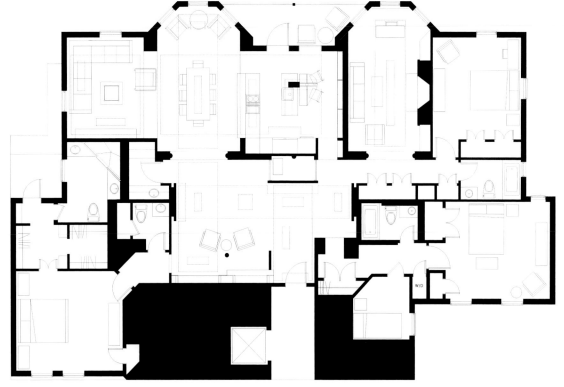

After

PREVIOUS PAGES: In the library and dining rooms, bold colors and dramatic lighting give a modern feel to this classic apartment. RIGHT: A view from the current dining room into the windowless library, the former dining room

Perspective Drawing

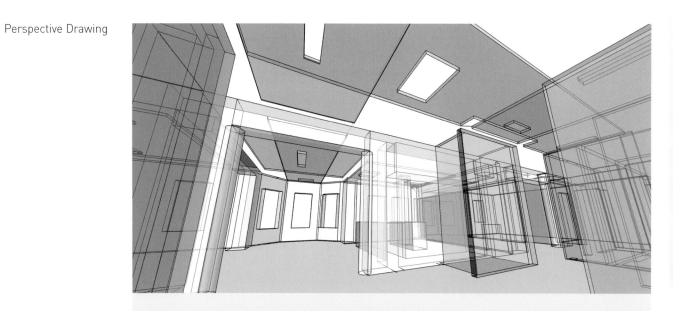

LEFT, ABOVE AND RIGHT:
Mahogany cabinetry and Absolute
Black granite finish the kitchen.
The floors throughout the
apartment are made of bamboo.

ABOVE AND FAR RIGHT: All
cabinetry in the apartment was
custom-designed by the the
architect. New freestanding
walls accommodate a large
art collection.

SULLIVAN STREET LOFT

ARCHITECT **TINA MANIS ASSOCIATES** • PHOTOGRAPHER **BJÖRG MAGNEA**

2500 SQUARE FEET

THIS TOP-FLOOR LOFT BENEFITS FROM WINDOWS ON THREE sides as well as from strategically placed skylights. The result is an exceptionally sunny apartment made even brighter by the use of sliding translucent doors and etched mirrors. The basic design strategy was to situate all of the public spaces along the window walls while placing storage and private areas against the apartment's windowless fourth wall.

The long, rectangular space narrows at the center where the kitchen is located. Behind it are the master bathroom and a powder room that share an open shower and bath but can be separated by sliding translucent doors. An etched mirror extends the full length of the bathroom.

A full-size opaque sliding panel separates the kitchen area from the master bedroom suite to create privacy.

PREVIOUS PAGES: The living and dining areas as seen from the entrance

RIGHT: The open kitchen features Basaltina stone counters and back-painted glass backsplashes.

Floor Plan

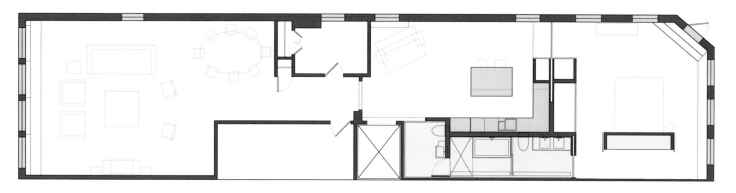

Perspectives

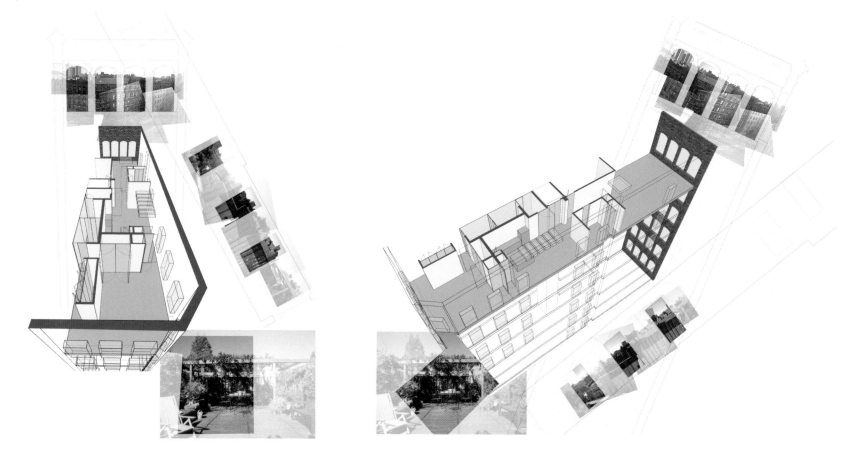

LEFT: A view of the kitchen; the door separating the kitchen from the master bedroom suite is shown partially closed.

RIGHT: In the master bedroom, the bed rests against a freestanding closet.

LEFT AND RIGHT: An etched mirror with cove lighting runs the length of the bathroom.

MEATPACKING DISTRICT LOFT

ARCHITECT **COLVIN DESIGN** • PHOTOGRAPHER **ELIZABETH FELICELLA**

2500 SQUARE FEET

LOCATED AT THE EDGE OF MANHATTAN'S MEATPACKING DISTRICT, this second-floor loft occupies part of a redisdential unit created by combining and converting several industrial buildings.

During the renovation, an existing brick wall with arches and cast-iron columns that support one-hundred-year-old steel-edged wooden beams were left untouched.

To bring light and a sense of expansiveness into the entry, the architect designed a maple-veneer "box" framed by clear glass. The interior of this "box" provids storage while the glass wall and clerestory allow sightlines into other spaces. The public areas, while open, are clearly defined by the use of such architectural elements as extended stone windowsills, cast-iron columns, and stone-topped counters.

The open kitchen/living/dining area is surrounded by custom millwork cabinets. Furniture "floats" on neutral area rugs, visually enlarging the space. The study has niches that contain floating maple bookshelves and indirect lighting. Unused loft doors became desks. The original brick wall separates off the master bedroom, providing a sense of privacy there.

Floor Plan

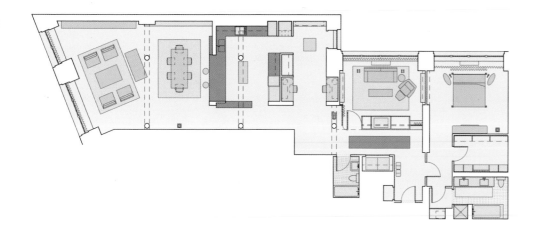

PREVIOUS PAGES: The living and dining area; existing iron columns and one-hundred-year-old wooden beams were left exposed.
LEFT: A view into the study
RIGHT: A view of the maple-veneer "box" surrounded by glass. The box acts as a space divider as a storage unit.

ABOVE: The study, where the original brick wall is exposed

RIGHT: A view of the kitchen from the dining area

LEFT: The living and dining
areas; the kitchen is to the right.
BELOW: The master bedroom

KELLNER LOFT

ARCHITECT **GARY SHOEMAKER ARCHITECTS, KINARI DESIGN** • PHOTOGRAPHER **EDUARD HUEBER/ARCHPHOTO**

2250 **SQUARE FEET**

EACH APARTMENT IN THIS BUILDING OCCUPIES AN ENTIRE FLOOR; as a result, one enters into this loft directly from the elevators. The secure entryway consists of a small foyer and a transclucent glass and aluminum façade. An arching blue wall, stopping several feet short of the ceiling, distinguishes the open space behind the façade. The wall, made of integral colored plaster, terminates at a raised aluminum platform that continues to trace the arc in plan. This platform distinguishes the living area and raises the sight line to the center of the window openings.

Tucked behind the wall is the master bedroom and bathroom, where sliding glass doors provide privacy. The master bathroom is defined by the glazed cube-shaped shower. The vanity and shower are comprised of the same integral colored plaster used for the arching wall. The shower is adjacent to the main entryway but it is separated by translucent glass that allows for a bit of voyeurism upon entering the loft.

On the opposite side of the apartment are a guest room, bathroom, and the kitchen, which opens to the dining area.

Floor Plan

PREVIOUS PAGES: The living area rests on a raised aluminum platform. RIGHT: The entry is via double aluminum and glass doors. The arching wall runs the length of the apartment, creating a dramatic entry into the gallery while enclosing the master bedroom.

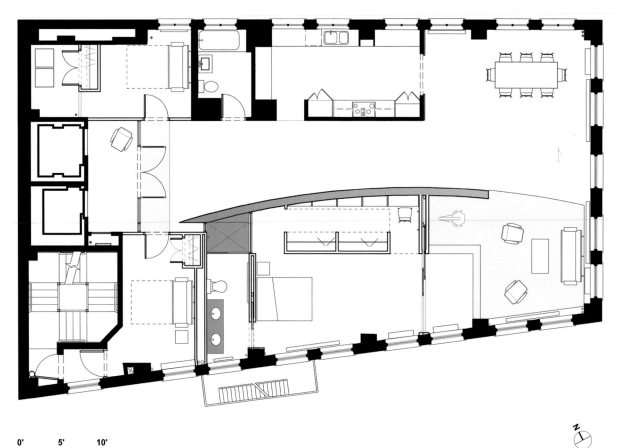

0'   5'   10'

Sections

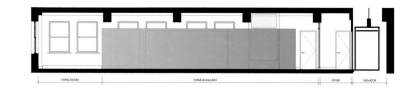

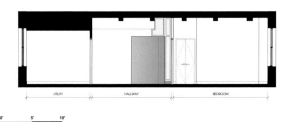

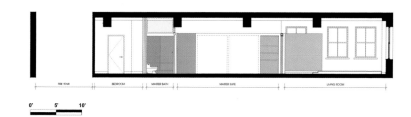

0'   5'   10'

0'   5'   10'

ABOVE: The arching wall is between the entry to the master bedroom and the entry to the loft.

RIGHT: A sweeping view of the loft, from the living area to the entry to the kitchen.

LEFT AND RIGHT: In the master bathroom, the vanity and shower are constructed of integral color plaster.

LEFT: A view of the master bedroom and bathroom from the living area

RIGHT: The master bedroom and living area, as seen from the master bathroom

SOHO DUPLEX

ARCHITECT DAVID HOTSON ARCHITECT • PHOTOGRAPHER EDUARD HUEBER/ARCHPHOTO

1800 SQUARE FEET

THE DESIGN STRATEGY FOR THIS RENOVATION WAS TO CAPITALIZE on the apartment's large front windows by creating a generous, double-height living room there that would enable that light to penetrate the bedrooms, kitchen, and dining area in the rear. To achieve this, any partitions needed to separate these rooms from the sunny living space were fashioned from etched glass panels and framed in satin aluminum: their hinged leaves allow the rooms to open directly into the double-height main space. At the mezzanine level, the floor that joins the media room to the two children's bedrooms was configured as a laminated-glass bridge passing over the dining area. Light fixtures were fitted into its translucent walls and floor for even more brightness. A new central air-conditioning system, concealed in the built-out party wall to conserve ceiling height, now freshens the interior rooms.

Architecturally, the project is rendered as a series of clearly defined, interpenetrating volumes. The principal space, the high-ceilinged living area, is defined by full-height walls on three sides and on the fourth side by the glass-and-aluminum mezzanine railings and the overhanging upper-level bedroom. Secondary spaces, including the dining area, kitchen, media room, and bridge, are sheathed in glass.

Upper Level Plan

PREVIOUS PAGES: View of dining,
kitchen, and living areas plus
underside of upper-level bridge
RIGHT: View of stairway to the
upper level with connecting bridge

Lower Level Plan

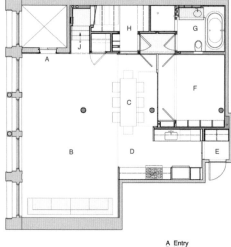

A Entry
B Living
C Dining
D Kitchen
E Service Entrance
F Master Bedroom
G Master Bath
H Dressing Area
J Stair
K Media Room
L Glass Bridge
M Bedroom
N Bathroom

ABOVE: The dining area's translucent walls bring light into the bedroom.
RIGHT: The kitchen

BELOW: Detail of bridge
LEFT: The glass bridge leads to the media room.

WHITE STREET LOFT

ARCHITECT **ANDRE KIKOSKI** • PHOTOGRAPHER **PETER AARON/ESTO**

1900 **SQUARE FEET**

THE FORMER STUDIO OF A WELL-KNOWN ARTIST, THIS LOFT HAS one hundred feet of windows along the front and side that figured prominently in its redesign for a family. Though the two bedrooms and bathrooms abut a windowless wall, the bedrooms are bathed in natural light because the operable panels that separate them from the sunny corridor are made of prismatic glass, architectural bronze, and mahogany. These panels can be opened for dramatic spaciousness or closed for warm intimacy.

The loft contains an eclectic mix of furnishings. Some pieces were designed by the architects while others are classic modern pieces; family heirlooms of Mayflower provenance share space with unique finds from around the globe.

A state-of-the-art cook's kitchen overlooks the loft's public spaces and also provides a sweeping view of the surrounding neighborhood. In the bathrooms, French limestone creates a warm spalike appearance. Topping it all off is an integrated stereo system, equipping this exceptionally bright space for both entertaining and daily living.

Floor Plan

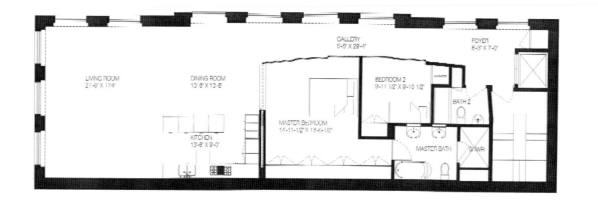

LIVING ROOM
21'-6" X 17'4"

DINING ROOM
13'-6" X 13'-6"

GALLERY
5'-5" X 29'-1"

FOYER
6'-3" X 7'-0"

BEDROOM 2
9'-11 1/2" X 9'-10 1/2"

BATH 2

KITCHEN
13'-6" X 9'-0"

MASTER BEDROOM
14'-11-1/2" X 13'-6-1/2"

MASTER BATH

SHWR

PREVIOUS PAGES: A commanding view of the apartment and the outdoors, as seen from the open kitchen.
BELOW: The kitchen
RIGHT: View of the dining and kitchen areas from the living area

PREVIOUS PAGES: Master
bedroom with a view down the
gallery to the entry foyer. The
sliding glass walls bring light
into the bedroom and allow the
loft to be completely open when

the owners are entertaining.
ABOVE: Master bedroom with a
view of the master bathroom
RIGHT: Master bathroom faced
with French limestone

BARNHARDT RESIDENCE

ARCHITECT **SIMPLE BROWN DESIGN** • PHOTOGRAPHER **RON POLLARD**

2500 SQUARE FEET

THIS FIFTH-FLOOR SPACE IS CARVED OUT OF A FORMER FLOUR mill located in Denver's Lower Downtown (LoDo). It incorporates three silos that were converted into the master bedroom, two bathrooms, and guestroom/office, respectively. These silos connect to the building proper, which houses the residence's living, dining, and kitchen areas. Finishing materials there include a leather floor inset with padded carpet, leather treads, recycled old-growth countertops, and custom steel shelving and rails. Custom-designed hot-rolled steel bookcases extend the length of this public space and act as a second skin for the room. Perforated steel panels backed by blued steel enclose built-in cabinets.

The westernmost silo contains the master bedroom, which has views of the Platte River. The closets were carefully designed to accentuate the curved walls while providing maximum storage. They are illuminated from above via round glass apertures that take advantage of indirect light bouncing to the ceiling. A woven wood screen provides privacy as well as a backdrop to the built-in headboard and end tables. A limestone stairway leads to the private steeping tub in the middle silo's master bath. The French limestone flooring there was laid upside down to take advantage of its rough surface. A private office that doubles as a guest room is located in the eastern silo. Walls within the silos stop short of the ceiling to reinforce the cylindrical shape of the silo and to lend a feeling of the expansiveness.

B

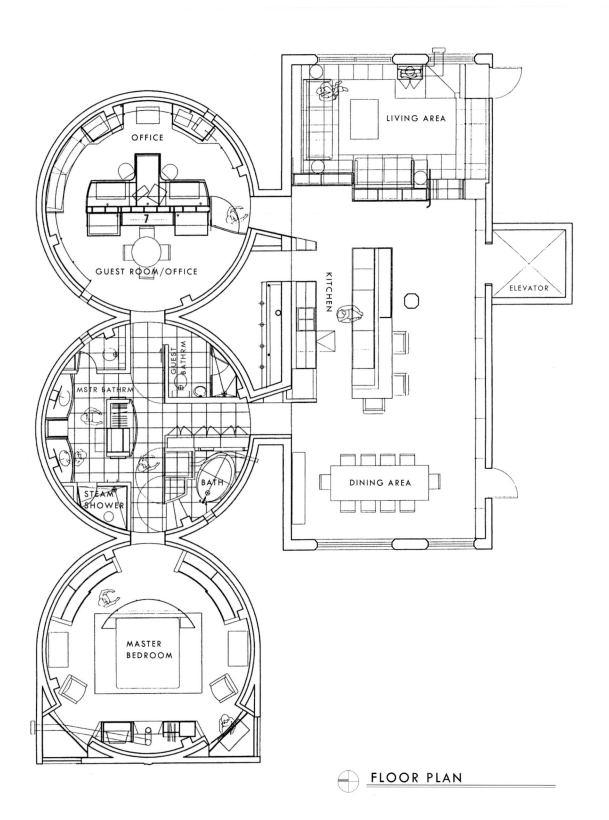

OFFICE

GUEST ROOM/OFFICE

LIVING AREA

ELEVATOR

KITCHEN

MSTR BATHRM

GUEST BATHRM

BATH

STEAM SHOWER

DINING AREA

MASTER BEDROOM

FLOOR PLAN

ABOVE LEFT: View from
the master bathroom to the
master bedroom
ABOVE RIGHT: View from the
office to the living area

LEFT: The living area is situated on a raised platform to take advantage of the cityscape views.
RIGHT: A view into the study

LEFT: The master bedroom
ABOVE: The master bathroom

ATHERLEY LOFT

ARCHITECT GARY SHOEMAKER ARCHITECTS • PHOTOGRAPHER EDUARD HUEBER/ARCHPHOTO

2300 SQUARE FEET

THE DESIRE FOR A MINIMALIST WHITE SPACE INSPIRED THE DESIGN of this apartment. With three exposures—north, south, and east—the 2,300-square-foot space is bathed with sunlight all day long. Within the space, the architect's design distinguishes between public and private areas very subtly, allowing each room to flow into the next. Edges of rooms or spaces are either blurred or sharply defined depending on the season and time of day. The large open living/dining area, featuring a double-sided fireplace, takes full advantage of the corner views and light.

A long gallery at the entry displays the owner's extensive photography collection. White epoxy floors and white painted walls and ceilings establish the minimalist look. Aluminum and stainless-steel accents such as the kitchen countertops, appliances, hardware, and light fixtures add visual layers to the project. Frosted green glass and aluminum sliding panels set off the master suite, while clear- and green-glass tiles adorn the centrally positioned shower in the master bath.

The client, interior designer Doug Atherley, made significant contributions to the project, collaborating on the furniture and fixture selections.

PREVIOUS PAGES:
BELOW: The entry foyer
RIGHT: The fireplace and
dining area as seen from
the living area

Floor Plan

Sections

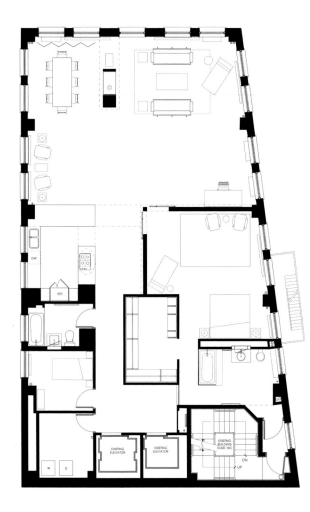

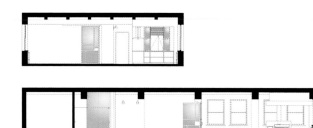

LEFT: The design of the master bathroom adheres to the apartment's minimalist style with tiles and shower walls all made of glass.
ABOVE: Master bedroom

GARDNER LOFT

ARCHITECT VALERIO DEWALT TRAIN ASSOCIATES • PHOTOGRAPHER STEVE HALL/HEDRICH BLESSING

2500 SQUARE FEET

BECAUSE OF EXTREME TIME PRESSURES, THE ARCHITECTS HAD one weekend to come up with a design for this unrenovated loft that could be executed within thirty days. A minimalist environment was the primary objective. The apartment shell was considered a blank white space. Within this shell were placed several overscale sculptural frames. These sculptural elements, made of galvanized sheet metal, had been fabricated and completely preassembled off-site, then shipped to the loft for installation. Nearly 3,000 components were lifted into the apartment by crane through the large windows. An plan of assembly had been prepared in advance.

The sculptural frames shape the interior space. Each form collides with others to suggest tension while each element also deliberately includes certain flaws: dents, bends, and folds. The frames delineate the kitchen and an office area, house audio visual equipment, and provide storage. Yet when their panels slide or swing shut, the rationale for each element is no longer obvious and the composition becomes perfectly abstract.

PREVIOUS PAGES: The living room is surrounded by galvanized sheet-metal forms that define the space and provide storage.

RIGHT: The apartment was seen as a white box within which space-defining elements were assembled.

Floor Plan

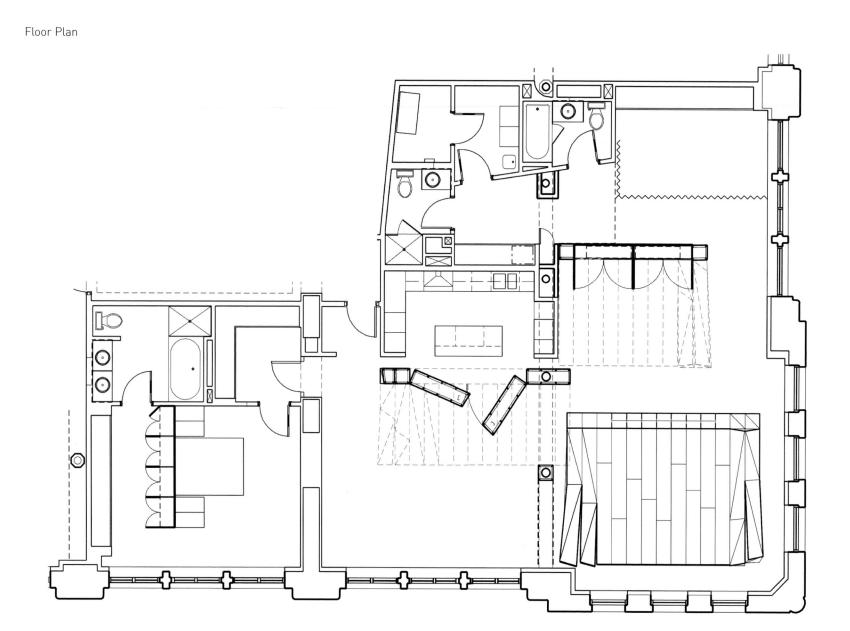

FAR LEFT: A view of the dining area with the living area beyond
LEFT: Minimalist furnishings complement the stark white and galvanized steel interior.

RIGHT: A view of the kitchen
from the dining area
FAR RIGHT: Looking toward the
dining area from the study area

LEFT: The master bedroom
RIGHT: A study area is carefully concealed within one of the galvanized steel storage units.

19TH STREET APARTMENT

ARCHITECT NANDINEE PHOOKAN ARCHITECT • **PHOTOGRAPHER** CHRISTOPHER WESNOFSKE

2500 SQUARE FEET

THE OWNERS OF THIS LOFT, A COUPLE WITH A YOUNG CHILD, WERE interested in a look that was clean and modern, imbued with the quiet, meditative quality associated with Asian design. While they wanted the apartment to maximize the open space for living and entertaining, they also needed separate, private spaces. One result of this principle: the home office, an extension of the main living space, was designed so that it could be closed off when necessary.

The private rooms were kept small but can open up completely to the living space through the use of sliding panels. Panels constructed of aluminum and glass surround the kitchen and office area when required. Quartersawn teak-veneer sliding panels separate the bedrooms from the hallway, through the child's bedroom can be opened to extend the play area into the corridor. Rich dark-brown leather panels can slide closed to create a guest bedroom next to the living area. The home office is a glass box within the spaces.

Jatoba wood flooring is used throughout the apartment. In the bathrooms, teak cabinetry is set off by limestone counters and floors.

Floor Plan

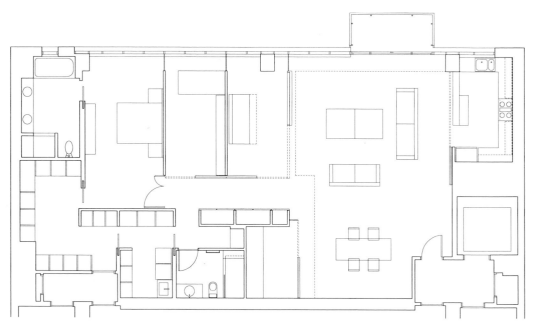

PREVIOUS PAGES: Panels of
glass, aluminum, and leather
allow the space within the loft
to be reconfigured.
RIGHT: A view of the guest bedroom
off the living area, separated by
leather-covered panels

RIGHT: A view from the living area of the kitchen; the home office is behind the aluminum-and-glass panels.

BELOW: Detail of bridge
LEFT: The glass bridge leads to the media room.

MORGAN LOFT

ARCHITECT **TANG KAWASAKI STUDIO** • PHOTOGRAPHER **BJÖRG MAGNEA**

2200 **SQUARE FEET**

THE PRIMARY DESIGN OBJECTIVES WERE TO EFFICIENTLY MAXIMIZE livable square footage and bring the tree-filtered light from south-facing windows as deep as possible into the loft. The clients' desire for a functional, simple space encouraged a reductive approach that incorporated the richly textured existing materials such as vaulted clay-brick ceilings and stained flatsawn white-oak floors.

The entire apartment is conceived of as an uninterrupted space in which public and private zones are separated by two massive white plaster walls. The walls conceal storage and contain niches for seating, for the bed, and even for fireplace logs. All architectural hardware, such as hinges and door pulls, is concealed, leaving seamless white surfaces to contrast with the brick walls and ceiling.

The kitchen features thick, seamless stainless-steel counters and glossy lacquered cabinet doors. Incandescent glass globes provide soft fill light.

Floor Plan

PREVIOUS PAGES: The rough, vaulted brick ceilings provide texture in the otherwise minimalist space

Kitchen Details

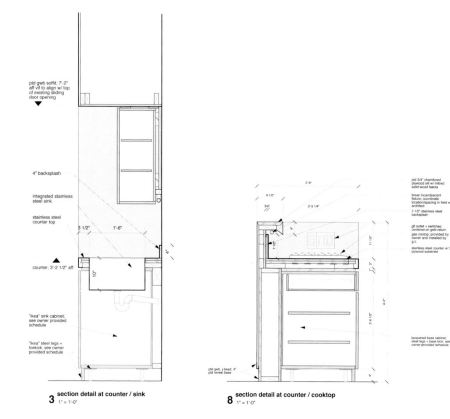

ptd gwb soffit; 7'-2" aff vif to align w/ top of existing sliding door opening

4" backsplash

integrated stainless steel sink

stainless steel counter top

3 1/2"   1'-6"

counter; 3'-2 1/2" aff.

10"

"ikea" sink cabinet; see owner provided schedule

"ikea" steel legs + toekick; see owner provided schedule

3 section detail at counter / sink
1" = 1'-0"

2'-9"

6 1/2"   2'-5 1/4"

3/4"

7 1/2"   11'-0"   4"

2'-2 1/2"

ptd gwb; j-bead; 4" ptd reveal base

ptd 3/4" chamfered plywood sill w/ mitred solid wood fascia

linear incandescent fixture; coordinate location/spacing in field w/ architect

7-1/2" stainless steel backsplash

gfi outlet + switches; centered on gwb return

gas cooktop; provided by owner and installed by g.c.

stainless steel counter w/ 3/4" plywood substrate

lacquered base cabinet; steel legs + base kick; see owner-provided schedule

8 section detail at counter / cooktop
1" = 1'-0"

Bathroom Details

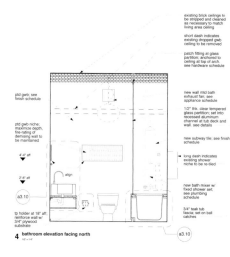

existing brick ceilings to be stripped and cleaned as necessary to match living area ceiling

short dash indicates existing dropped gwb ceiling to be removed

patch fitting at glass partition; anchored to ceiling at top of arch. see hardware schedule

new wall mtd bath exhaust fan; see appliance schedule

1/2" thk. clear tempered glass partition; set into recessed aluminum channel at tub deck and wall. see details

new subway tile; see finish schedule

long dash indicates existing shower niche to be re-tiled

new bath mixer w/ fixed shower set; see plumbing schedule

3/4" teak tub fascia; set on ball catches

ptd gwb; see finish schedule

ptd gwb niche; maximize depth, fire-rating of demising wall to be maintained

4'-4" aff

2'-6" aff

a3.10

tp holder at 18" aff; reinforce wall w/ 3/4" plywood substrate

align

bottom of pendant; 7'-2" aff

4 bathroom elevation facing north
1/2" = 1'-0"

a3.10

5 bathroom elevation facing east
1/2" = 1'-0"

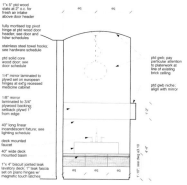

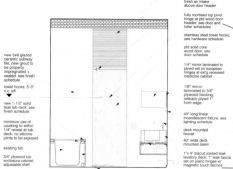

new 3x6 glazed ceramic subway tile; new grout to be properly impregnated + sealed. see finish schedule

towel hooks; 5'-0" o.c. aff

new 1-1/2" solid teak tub deck; see finish schedule

minimize use of caulking to within 1/4" reveal at tub deck; no silicone joints to be exposed

existing tub

3/4" plywood tub enclosure cabinet; adjustable shelf

1"x 5" ptd wood slats at 2" o.c. for fresh air intake above door header

fully mortised top pivot hinge at ptd wood door header; see door and hdwr schedules

stainless steel towel hooks; see hardware schedule

ptd solid core wood door; see door schedule

1/4" mirror laminated to plywd set on european hinges at extg recessed medicine cabinet

1/8" mirror laminated to 3/4" plywood backing; setback plywd 1" from edge

40" long linear incandescent fixture; see lighting schedule

deck mounted faucet

40" wide deck mounted basin

1"x 4" biscuit jointed teak lavatory deck; 1" teak fascia set on piano hinges w/ magnetic touch latches

ptd gwb; pay particular attention to platework at line of existing brick ceiling

ptd gwb niche; align with mirror

Sections

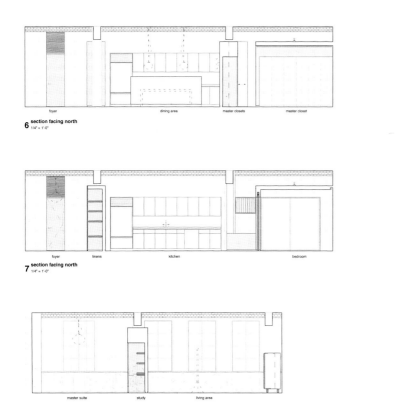

6 section facing north
1/4" = 1'-0"

foyer · dining area · master closets · master closet

7 section facing north
1/4" = 1'-0"

foyer · linens · kitchen · bedroom

8 section facing south
1/4" = 1'-0"

master suite · study · living area

Sections

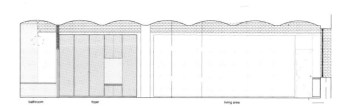

1 section facing east
1/4" = 1'-0"

bathroom · foyer · living area

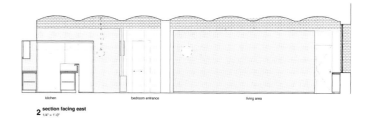

2 section facing east
1/4" = 1'-0"

kitchen · bedroom entrance · living area

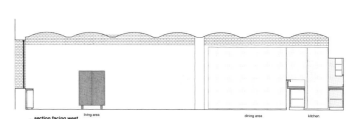

3 section facing west
1/4" = 1'-0"

living area · dining area · kitchen

Cabinet Details

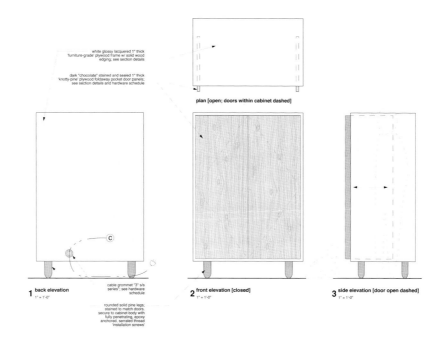

white glossy lacquered 1" thick 'furniture-grade' plywood frame w/ solid wood edging; see section details

dark "chocolate" stained and sealed 1" thick 'knotty-pine' plywood foldaway pocket door panels; see section details and hardware schedule

plan [open; doors within cabinet dashed]

1 back elevation
1" = 1'-0"

cable grommet "3" s/s series"; see hardware schedule

rounded solid pine legs; stained to match doors; secure to cabinet body with fully penetrating, epoxy anchored, serrated thread 'installation screws'

2 front elevation [closed]
1" = 1'-0"

3 side elevation [door open dashed]
1" = 1'-0"

RIGHT: Similarly, the fireplace and wood storage appear to be carved out of another wall.
FAR RIGHT: A niche for the bed is carved out of a thick wall that contains storage

CHELSEA APARTMENT

ARCHITECT **ARCHITECTURE IN FORMATION** • PHOTOGRAPHER **MATTHEW BREMER**

1200 SQUARE FEET

ONCE AN AWKWARD TWO-BEDROOM SPACE, THIS IMPLICIT apartment was reconfigured to create more usable rooms with improved flow between them. One of the clients is a chef, so the design of the kitchen and its relationship to the rest of the apartment was an important consideration. It was enlarged and opened up to the living and dining areas. A mirrored backsplash reflects the view of the living area and reuses light from the dining area windows.

The separate living room and dining room were combined and the dining area was moved to the front of the loft, along the window wall. A Spanish cedar closet at the end of the entry defines the edge of the kitchen and living room. This custom closet is visible from all sides and is lit from within, which creates a glow between the wooden slats. The existing second bedroom was converted into a lounge with a built-in desk. The single bathroom was split into a master bath with a Venetian plaster shower and a smaller guest bathroom.

PREVIOUS PAGES: View of the
living area with the cedar closet
as seen from the dining area
RIGHT: View of the living area
from the entry hall
BELOW: Entry

Floor Plan

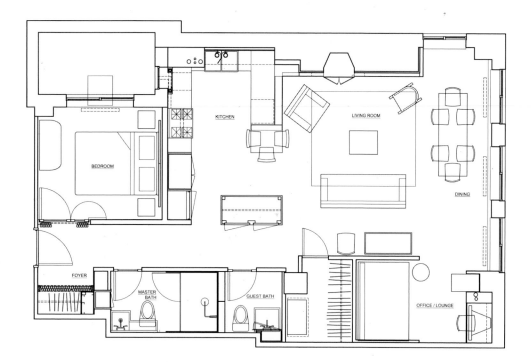

BEDROOM

KITCHEN

LIVING ROOM

DINING

FOYER

MASTER
BATH

GUEST BATH

OFFICE / LOUNGE

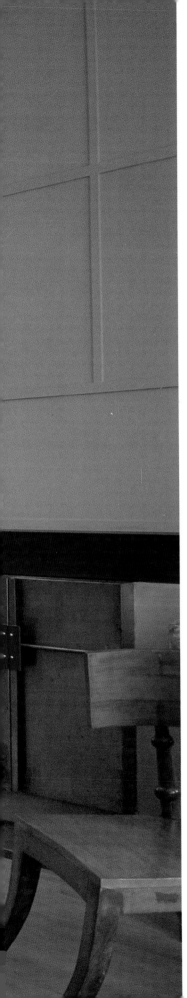

LEFT: Kitchen sink detail
FAR LEFT: The mercury-etched mirror in the kitchen reflects light from the living/dining area windows.

ABOVE: Master bathroom
with stainless-steel vanity
LEFT: Guest nook
RIGHT: Master bedroom

ZARTOSHTY RESIDENCE

ARCHITECT **STEPHEN CHUNG AND KAMRAN ZAHEDI/URBANICA** • PHOTOGRAPHER **ERIC ROTH**

2400 SQUARE FEET

THIS PROJECT INVOLVED THE CONVERSION OF 2,400 SQUARE FEET of raw space into a primary residence for a young bachelor. The owner wanted a home that would be ideal for frequent entertaining, including large gatherings. As a result, the design incorporates a double-height living/dining area, an open kitchen, a wet bar, and a media room. Sliding wooden doors allow the media room to be closed off for private viewing. All of the public areas are on the lower level, while the master bedroom and bathroom and a study loft are on the upper level.

The finishing materials are carefully chosen for their luxurious look and strong architectural expression. All of the cabinetry, doors, and trim, and most of the flooring, is dark walnut with a matte finish. Some walls, the counters, and the floors are a light beige travertine. Stairway guardrails and cabinet and shower doors are sandblasted glass. Other walls are rendered in veneer plaster with semigloss paint. Mirrors placed strategically throughout the space provide unexpected visual effects.

Upper Level

Lower Level

PREVIOUS PAGES: A view of the living room from the dining area

RIGHT: Perspective drawing of the living and dining areas and the kitchen

BELOW RIGHT: Detail of fireplace with beige travertine

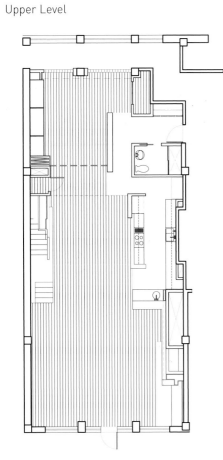

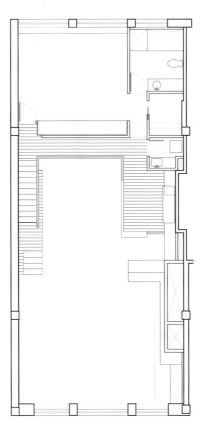

Section

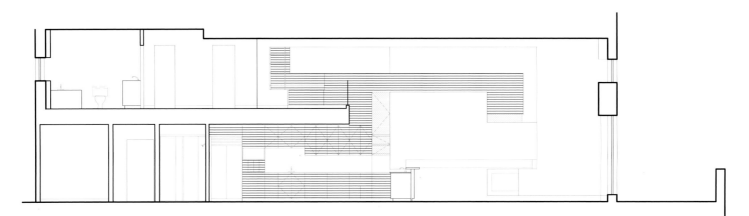

LEFT: The dining area and kitchen with the media room beyond

ABOVE: The upper-level study
RIGHT: The kitchen

GORDON SOHO SKYLINE LOFT

ARCHITECT **DEAN/WOLF ARCHITECTS** • PHOTOGRAPHER **JEFF GOLDBERG/ESTO**

2350 SQUARE FEET

THIS LOFT WAS DESIGNED TO COMPLEMENT THE SURROUNDING skyline. Amplifying the extreme linearity of the steel-and-concrete building, the public room incorporates the cityscape, acting as a "stage" for the occupants, and the indoor shadows and reflections of the metropolis take on as much importance as the constructed elements.

The interplay between the windows and the reflective glass walls nearby turns a procession through the space into a passage between two skylines—one real, the other virtual and ephemeral. At the same time, tactile cabinetry denotes areas away from the public stage, holding the private spaces of a child's bunk beds, a master-bedroom table, and a study desk.

A line of light penetrates these deep recesses, capturing morning sun and creating an intimate link between inhabitants.

Floor Plan

Conceptual Drawings

PREVIOUS PAGES: View of the entry, living area, and kitchen RIGHT: The maple kitchen counter is constructed as a series of layers, with work space at one end and dining space at the other.

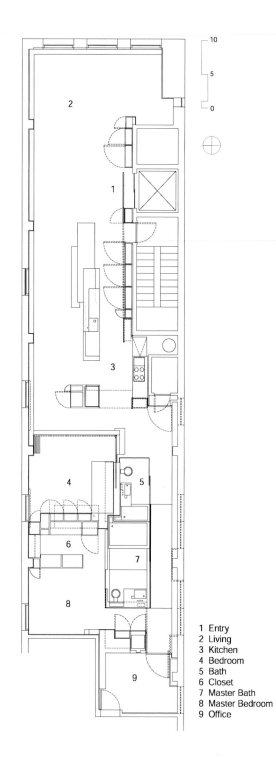

1 Entry
2 Living
3 Kitchen
4 Bedroom
5 Bath
6 Closet
7 Master Bath
8 Master Bedroom
9 Office

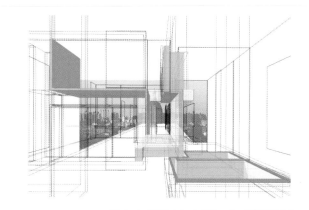

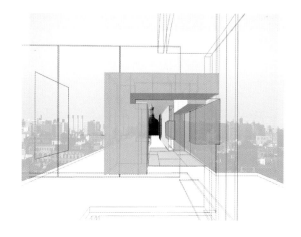

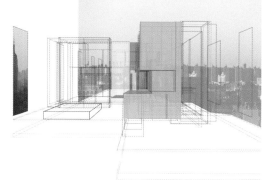

LEFT: The kitchen features maple plywood cabinetry.

ABOVE: Two views of the
master bathroom
RIGHT: Master bedroom

MIDTOWN TRIPLEX

ARCHITECT AJS DESIGNS • PHOTOGRAPHER BJÖRG MAGNEA

800 SQUARE FEET

THE TRIPLEX'S MOST DRAMATIC ELEMENT IS EIGHTEEN-FOOT, vertical space that had been concealed by the previous layout. Moving the kitchen away to another section of the center level exposed all three floors as well as the vertical space that joins them. The resulting interior tower contains the stairway and is punctuated with an etched glass opening and drywall brow at the upper-level master bedroom.

The design of the stair provides a sense of connection and vertical movement. The maple steps and risers form a blond ziggurat that lightens in scale as they ascend. In the lower-level living room the stairs tie into the adjacent cabinetry. Above, they delicately bridge the two floors.

To refine the lines of the space, the architect massed a number of functional elements together. For example, the master bath's door had been opposite the bed and directly in front of the toilet. Since the toilet could not be moved, the door was relocated next to the door of an adjacent closet. Both became pocket doors enclosed in a single frame, at once making the appearance both simpler and more substantial. Similarly, for the fireplace, ceramic tile melds the hearth with the space where the HVAC unit is located.

PREVIOUS PAGES: A view looking down to the living room from the elevated dining area

RIGHT: The study area, part of the lower-level living room

Upper Level Plan

Lower Level Plan

Center Level Plan

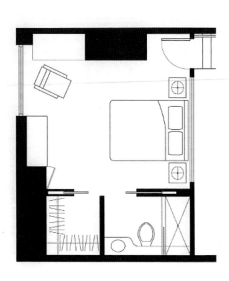

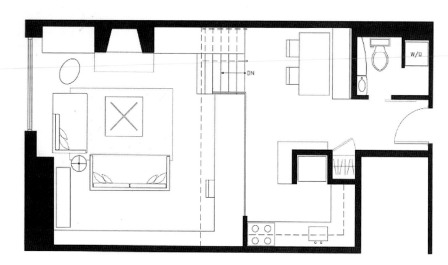

Sections

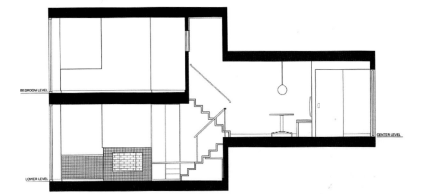

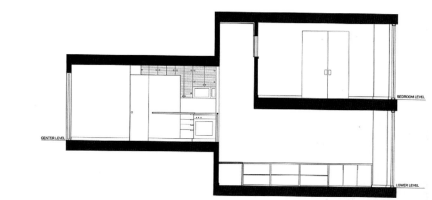

LEFT: The dining area
FAR LEFT: A view of the kitchen from the dining area

LEFT: The powder room
RIGHT: The master bedroom with sandblasted glass facing the stairwell tower

CAPPS LOFT

ARCHITECT **POTEET ARCHITECTS/FAB ARCHITECTURE** • PHOTOGRAPHER **PAUL BARDAGJY**

2300 **SQUARE FEET**

THIS PROJECT IS LOCATED IN THE KING WILLIAM LOFTS, A CONVERSION of a century-old industrial complex in San Antonio's King William Historic District. The owner, a collector of contemporary art, wanted a space in which to display a growing collection.

The lower level is designed for entertaining—its public character is underscored by a large, uncovered steel window that opens onto a breezeway, allowing passersby to see in. This level also includes a full kitchen. A suspended cabinet above the kitchen island displays glassware and other objects.

The stairway to the upper level is enclosed at the foot; at the bottom landing, a tiny powder room is tucked behind a glazed door. The larger landing is expanded into a mezzanine, which serves as a home office. At this point the stair becomes an open steel structure leading to the upper level where there are two linear suites—one containing living area, media room, and guest bedroom and bath, the other with the master bedroom and bath plus dressing and utility areas. The living area contains a satellite kitchen/bar.

PREVIOUS PAGES: The living
and sitting areas
RIGHT: View of the stairs to the
living area from the lower kitchen
FAR RIGHT: View of the living
room from the upper kitchen

Main Level

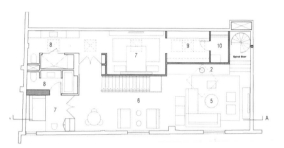

Mezzanine Level

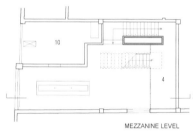

MEZZANINE LEVEL

Lower Level

Section

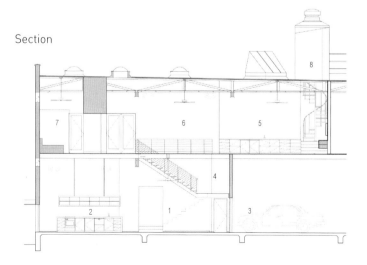

LEFT: View of kitchen from the mezzanine
RIGHT: View of stairs from lower kitchen

LEFT: Spiral stairs lead to a
private roof deck.

LEFT: The master bedroom
with the dressing room beyond
ABOVE: The master bath

COLLINS LOFT

ARCHITECT **DEAN/WOLF ARCHITECTS** • PHOTOGRAPHER **PETER AARON/ESTO**

1550 SQUARE FEET

THIS LOFT CONSISTS OF AN OPEN CENTER AND TWO CLUSTERS OF rooms, one private "interior" the other public "exterior." The center of each cluster is marked by a threshold, while the clusters are finished in different materials to emphasize their separateness from each other and the rest of the loft.

At one end of the loft a broad steel threshold anchors the entry, two studies (one enclosed, the other open), and the kitchen. The desk and kitchen island are constructed of the same steel, thereby unifying the space. In the loft's communal center, rough ceiling beams and exposed brick walls recall the space's earlier industrial use and contrast sharply with the steel and the dark walnut floors. At the other end of this space, a second threshold links the living room, the master suite, and the exterior deck. Here, the common material is concrete and cement boards. Echoing the concrete threshold, a series of full-height steel doors with cement-board face panels line the space.

PREVIOUS PAGES: The kitchen, dining, and living area with the entry to the master bedroom beyond
RIGHT: Ceiling and wall detail

FAR RIGHT: A steel threshold marks the entry to the area containing the enclosed study and the exterior study with steel desk.

Floor Plan

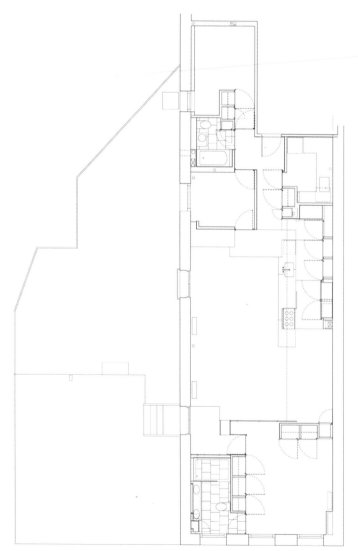

LEFT: A view toward the master
bedroom from the dining area,
with doors to the terrace on
the right
RIGHT: A view from the entry
to the kitchen, living and dining
areas, and studies